Michael O'Flanagan

GW01091211

# The
# Ingredients
# of
# Poetry

RIPOSTE BOOKS DUBLIN

First Published in 1999 by

# *RIPOSTE BOOKS*

28 Emmet Rd., Dublin 8. Ireland


Cover by  the author.
Printed by  PRINTECH INTERNATIONAL

ISBN 1 901596 01 X

# Contents

In Memory of my late aunt
ROSELEEN RYAN
Ar Dheis Dé Go Raibh a Anam Dílis

# Acknowledgements

*I would like to express my gratitude to Liam O'Meara for his invaluable assistance during the preparation of this book. Also to Lynda Grimes for technical assistance. To the members of Syllables whose company I have enjoyed over ten years, to the members of Riposte who have given me permission to include their work and whose friendship and support I've enjoyed over the last four years. Also to my wife Helena whose fortitude has enabled her to survive nearly thirty years in close proximity, to me.*

*I would also like to acknowledge the co-operation of The Kilmainham Arts Conference, The Dublin Writers' Workshop, The Dublin Writers' Centre, The Rathmines Writers' Workshop, Poetry Ireland, Resonance Writers, Poetry Plus, Chapter and Verse, North Clare Writers' Group, Shannon Writers' Group, Killybegs Writers' Group, Granard Writers' Group, Wexford Writers' Group, Belfast Writers' Group, St Colm Cill Writers' Group and Virgina House Writers whose support has been essential to the success of the Riposte experiment.*

# *Introduction*

## The Importance of Poetry

Poetry is something of a puzzle in modern life. Whereas in former times only the elite and those wholly immersed in literature would dare to resort to poetry (i.e. to illustrate a point in debate or to mark a special event ) now most lay persons are willing to recite their favourite four lines on the slimmest pretext. And yet there is a feeling that poetry is no longer held in much awe, that good and bad poetry is treated with equal respect (or lack of it) and that poetry generally, is regarded as just another throw-away consumer product. Could it be that that the ingredients of today's poetry, like the ingredients of so many other modern products, have been down-graded in value. Plastic replacing wood, ever lighter metals, cardboard- fibreglass. Surely we cannot be happy to equate reading a poem with eating a TV dinner? It must be, that poetry can offer an alternative to all that cheapens modern life. When we contemplate the "word" we contemplate meaning. For the most part, poetry is not distracted by music, movement or tempo. It is a catalyst to contemplation and reflection and the very sparseness of the topics contained in most poetry urge us to examine in detail the beauty of objects which we often casually disregard in other moods. Spending a few minutes reading a poem, or writing one, can equate to a mini-retreat in a time when we know that not everyone can withdraw to a monastery at the weekends. So where does the urge to write poetry come from? It might be that people have more time, ( that's doubtful with so many modern distractions ) but many thousands more are resorting to poetry as a pastime. More likely, it's a sense of dissatisfaction with the profusion of other entertainment's that spurs ever more people to write poetry today. Whether Art can be therapy or Therapy, art, has been a long standing debate but there is no denying that people more and more feel the need for both. Writing poetry provides a ready release for frustrations and many beginners have to surmount this phase before moving on to topics of a more general nature. But poems about the "human condition" have been universally popular in every age, and the stresses of modern life provide ample new area's to be explored. Poems of this nature can be satisfying when well written and can generate true empathy at the finest levels. Establishing empathy between human beings is one of the great facilities of poetry and here again this seems to be a quality that is seriously on the wane in today's world. From *Pope* to *Yeats,* from *Clough* to *Dylan Thomas* we find the readiness to contemplate the human condition, in ever varying ways, a suitable subject for poetry. Yet poetry is more than a whinge, - humour, beauty and the miracles of everyday life are well celebrated in poetry. Ballads and narrative poetry are much less popular now than in former times possibly because other media are more efficient at recording the events which formerly would have secured their permanence in poetry. So what then are the ingredients of poetry. People regularly debate the difference between prose and poetry, even more so now as the "*prose poem*" has become so popular in recent times.

# Prose And Poetry

It is difficult to say exactly where the difference lies between prose and poetry, especially in an era when the "prose poem" is paramount. It will be easier to point out the differences between a regular piece of prose and one of traditional poetry. These differences can best be illustrated by the following;

## Poem 1

I wandered lonely as a cloud
That floats on high o'er vales and hills,
When all at once I saw a crowd,
A host, of golden daffodils;
Beside the lake, beneath the Trees,
Fluttering and dancing in the breeze.

Continuous as the stars that shine,
And twinkle on the milky way,
They stretched in never-ending line
Along the margin of a bay:
Ten thousand saw I at a glance,
Tossing their heads in sprightly dance.

The waves beside them danced: but they
Out-did the sparkling waves in glee:
A poet could not but be gay
In such a jocund company:
I gazed-and gazed-but little thought
What wealth the show to me had brought:

For oft when on my couch I lie
In vacant or in pensive mood,
They flash upon that inward eye
Which is the bliss of solitude,
And then my heart with pleasure fills
And dances with the daffodils.

**Wm. Wordsworth**

*When we were in the woods beyond Gowbarrow Park we
saw a few daffodils close to the waterside. We fancied that
the sea had floated the seeds ashore, and that the little
colony had so sprung up.  But as we went along there were
more and yet more; at last under the boughs of the trees, we
saw that there was a long belt of them along the shore about
the breadth of a country turnpike road. I never saw daffodils
so beautiful. They grew among the mossy stones about and
above them; some rested their heads upon these stones, as
on a pillow, for weariness; and the rest tossed and reeled
and danced and seemed as if they verily laughed with the
wind, that blew upon them over the lake; they looked so gay,
ever glancing, ever changing. The wind blew directly over
the lake to them. There was here and there a little knot and
a few stragglers higher up; but they were so few as not to
disturb the simplicity, unity, and life of the one busy
highway.*

Dorothy Wordsworth

This poem and  piece of prose were written by a brother and
sister, William and Dorothy Wordsworth. It can be seen
immediately that both extracts deal with the same topic.
Dorothy Wordsworth's is a descriptive passage about
daffodils; William Wordsworth's is a poem about the same
daffodils. Both pieces deal with the same aspect of the topic,
describing the sudden appearance of a field of daffodils.
However there are many differences in style.  In the poetic
version there is no mention of the  Park, or of their feelings
on first seeing the flowers.  Wordsworth  does not include
these facts in his poem. One of the aims of prose is to give
information,    and    Dorothy    Wordsworth    names    the
countryside in order to enlighten us. The purpose of  poetry
is to excite a feeling of pleasure, wonder or even  surprise. In
the poem, therefore, mention of the definite place is omitted
and we are left to imagine the poet wandering through some

nameless but beautiful area. William Wordsworth goes on to say that he is wandering 'lonely as a cloud'; and continues to refer to himself as being alone. Yet we know from a journal kept by his sister, that this was not the case. Changing the facts like this, is called a poetic licence. Wordsworth tells at the end of the poem of the effect the sight had on him. He expresses his joy and delight that the sight gave him. A poem like this which deals with the poet's own feelings is called a *lyric*. The language in both the poem and the prose piece is quite simple ; in fact, nearly all the words used are in common use in everyday language. Still, this simple language expresses in the most powerful way, all of the facts. The reader's pleasure is enhanced by the way the poet commonly uses devices that are not so common in prose. Wordsworth is not satisfied to say he is lonely, he wants to give a deeper insight, so he says he was as *'lonely as a cloud'* This one word *cloud* helps *to* bring other ideas such as peace and beauty into play. They are a part of the scene he is describing, and so they fit well with his design. Again in the line *Continuous as the stars that shine,* he compares the mass of daffodils to the stars in the milky way. In this way he brings out not only the number of daffodils, but their freshness and dancing. This comparison of one thing with another is called a *simile*. A simile is introduced by the word *as* or *like*. The change from simple language to simile is called a Figure of Speech.

### METRE

Metre is a method of measuring the rhythm of a poem, by noting where syllables are stressed in various types of traditional poetry. If we read over the first two lines of the poem, putting a stress of the voice on the syllables that receive it and mark each accented syllable by - , the lines will read

> I wándered lónely ás a clóud
> That floáts on high o'er váles and hílls.

9

Every second syllable receives more stress or emphasis than the others. Let us mark each stressed syllable with the sign -, and each unstressed syllable with " The lines then appear as:

> Ï wándëred lónely as ä cloúd
> Thät flóats ön hígh över váles änd hílls.

We can now proceed to divide the syllables into groups that are repeated over and over again. In this way we can show the rhythm of the poem. Mark off each group with the sign / taking care to cut off the syllables accurately.

> Ï wán   /   dëred lóne   /   lÿ ás   /   ä cloúd
> Thät flóats   /   ön hígh   /   ö'er váles   /   änd hílls.

The measure is "-, that is, of two syllables, the first of which is not stressed, and the second is stressed.   Groups of syllables that repeat themselves in poetry are called *feet*. They are of several kinds, chiefly of two and three syllables, which are given different  names. The foot (" -)  is called an iamb or iambus, and the line composed of iambs is said to be an iambic line. Each of the above lines has *four* iambs in it. Lines are named from the number of feet, of whatever kind they contain: a line of four feet, for instance, is called a tetrameter, from the Greek words for *four* and *measure*. Now, since the line has four feet, each of which is an iamb, we call it an *iambic tetrameter*. Most traditional poetry rhymes-that is, it has an arrangement of words that conclude with a similar sound. As will be seen, rhyme is not necessary, though it is sometimes adds to the beauty of a poem. In this poem *cloud* rhymes with *crowd* and *hills* with *daffodils*.   The *ends* of the final words of each line are similar to each other. If we call the lines that rhyme together a, b, and c respectively, we have in each verse the arrangement
>                a b a b c c.
A group of lines that repeat in this way is called a *stanza*.

## Poem 2

He scarce had ceased when the superior fiend
Was moving toward the shore; his ponderous shield,
Ethereal temper, massy, large, and round,
Behind him cast; the broad circumference
Hung on his shoulders like the moon, whose orb
Through optic glass the Tuscan artist views
At evening, from the top of Fesole
Or in Valdarno, to descry new lands,
Rivers or mountains in her spotted globe.
His spear-to equal which the tallest pine,
Hewn on Norwegian hills to be the mast
Of some great Ammiral, were but a wand-
He walked with to support uneasy steps
Over the burning marle, not like those steps
On heaven's azure; and the torrid clime
Smote on him sore besides, vaulted with fire.
Natheless he so endured, till on the beach
Of that inflamèd sea, he stood, and called
His legions, Angel forms, who lay entranced,
Thick as autumnal leaves that strow the brooks
In Vallombrosa, where th' Etrurian shades
High overarched embower; or scattered sedge
Afloat, when with fierce winds Orion armed
Hath vexed the Red-sea coast, whose waves o'erthrew
Busiris and his Memphian chivalry,
While with perfidious hatred they pursued
The sojourners of Goshen, who beheld
From the safe shore their floating carcasses
And broken chariot wheels: so thick bestrown
Abject and lost lay these, covering the flood,
Under amazement of their hideous change.

MILTON,
*Paradise Lost*

This is an extract from an epic, that is, a poem dealing with a heroic event. In his epic Milton deals with the fall of Man, and this is a description of Satan, the head of the fallen angels. Everything in this poem is staggering. This is achieved by the use of powerful similes and the fearful and

11

terrible vistas of the burning lake and the hordes of fallen angels. Everything moves slowly. There is a lot of elaborate description which constantly adds to the length of the story. The aim of an epic therefore is to describe the vista, rather than to tell a story. The important point to note about this poem is the use of similes. These similes are not just figures of speech; they are important pieces of description in themselves. Milton compares Satan's shield to the moon as seen through a telescope, and then goes on to describe how the moon is seen, and what is seen. and by whom. He then goes on to describe the destruction of the Egyptian army.


The Metre.
Scan the lines as follows:

Hë scárce / häd móved, / whën thé / süpér / iör fiénd
Wäs móv/ ïng töwárd / thë shóre. / Hïs pónd / ëröus shiéld

Note there are *five* feet in each line, so each is a pentameter. The feet are chiefly iambs, so the line is an iambic pentameter *(5xa)*. The iambic pentameter receives the special name of *heroic line.* There is no rhyme, so the poem is said to be blank. The name *blank verse* is generally given to this metre namely, the heroic line.

# Poem 3

I see his blood upon the rose
And in the stars the glory of his eyes,
His body gleams amid eternal snows,
His tears fall from the skies.

I see his face in every flower
The thunder and the singing of the birds
Are but his voice-and carven by his power
Rocks are his written  words.

All pathways by his feet are worn,
His strong heart stirs the ever-beating sea,
His crown of thorns is twined with every thorn,
His cross is every tree.

Joseph Mary Plunket

In this poem the poet professes his belief in God. It was
written in an age when belief in God was the norm rather
than the exception. The poem is written in quatrains with a
rhyming pattern of  *a b a b*  throughout.  Not only does the
poem comprise a series of metaphors,  it is a search for
suitable figures of speech to glorify God. There is no doubt
entertained in this poem. Not only are the beliefs held firmly,
but they are stated as fact. e.g. *His tears fall from the skies*
leaves no room for debate. The entire poem is written in the
*declarative mood.* Poems of this style are often described as
dogmatic and yet, because of its simple style and pleasing
images, the poem effects satisfying a vista of  beauty.

## Poem 4

The yellow bittern that never broke out
In a drinking bout, might as well have drunk;
His bones are thrown on a naked stone
Where he lived alone like a hermit monk.
O yellow bittern! I pity your lot,
Though they say that a sot like myself is curst-
I was sober a while, but I'll drink and be wise
For I fear I should die in the end of thirst.
It's not for the common birds that I'd mourn,
The black-bird, the corn-crake, or the crane,
But for the bittern that's shy and apart
And drinks in the marsh from the lone bog-drain.
Oh! if I had known you were near your death,
While my breath held out I'd have run to you,
Till a splash from the Lake of the Son of the Bird
Your soul would have stirred and waked anew.
My darling told me to drink no more
Or my life would be o'er in a little short while;
But I told her 'tis drink gives me health and strength
And will lengthen my road by many a mile.
You see how the bird of the long smooth neck
Could get his death from the thirst at last-
Come, son of my soul, and drain your cup,
You'll get no sup when your life is past.
In a wintering island by Constantine's halls
A bittern calls from a wineless place,
And tells me that hither he cannot come
Till the summer is here and the sunny days.
When he crosses the stream there and wings o'er the sea
Then a fear comes to me he may fail in his flight-
Well, the milk and the ale are drunk every drop,
And a dram won't stop our thirst this night.

Thomas McDonagh

"The Yellow Bittern" is a poem in praise of drink, i.e. alcoholic drink. It's a translation from an older Irish song by Cathal Buidhe MacGiolla Ghunna which was sung on festive occasions when drink was the preoccupation of all those present. The Bittern was a shy bird which lived and quenched its thirst on the bog. It stayed away from inhabited places in contrast to most of the other birds. In the winter when the waterways were frozen, the other birds could still drink where humans had broken the ice; but the Bittern died in isolation because it could not get a drink. Despite the Bittern's death, the mood of the poem is one of celebration, the equivalent of *"eat, drink and be merry for tomorrow we die!"*

## Poem 5

# Thomas McDonagh

He shall not hear the bittern cry
In the wild sky where he is lain,
Nor voices of the sweeter birds
Above the wailing of the rain.

Nor shall he know when loud March blows
Thro' slanting snows her fanfare shrill,
Blowing to flame the golden cup
Of many an upset daffodil.

But when the Dark Cow leaves the moor,
And pastures poor with greedy weeds,
Perhaps he'll hear her low at morn
Lifting her horn in pleasant meads.

Francis Ledwidge

This poem is a *lament.* for Thomas McDonagh. Francis Ledwidge, Thomas McDonagh and Joseph Mary Plunket, were three poets and friends who were part of the poetry circle in Dublin from 1912 onwards. In 1916 McDonagh and Plunket were executed for their part in the Easter Week Rebellion. Ledwidge wrote laments for his two friends Plunket and McDonagh in 1916 and he himself was killed in The Great War, at Ypre in 1917.

In this lament Ledwidge refers to the Bittern, which was among McDonagh's better known works. Apart from the beauty of the rural images contained in the poem, it is remarkable for its use of mid-line rhyme which was a feature of ancient Irish poems written in the Irish language. The use of the image of " *The Dark Cow,* " a symbol for Ireland, also recalls the work of an earlier Irish poet, James Clarence Mangan.

# FIGURES OF SPEECH.

**Metaphor**. One thing is for the moment identified
with another.

*Rocks are his written words*

Joseph Mary Plunket,  I see his blood upon the rose

**Personification.**     A thing is turned into a person.

*For the Angel of Death spread his wings on the blast,*

Lord Byron   *Destruction of Sennacherib*

**Simile.**     One thing is compared to another.

*I wandered lonely as a cloud,*

William Wordsworth   *The Daffodils*

**Apostrophe.**     An address to a thing, or to a person,
that cannot reply.

*Oh1  Yellow Bittern I pity your lot,*

Thomas  McDonagh, The Yellow Bittern

**Exclamation**.

A sudden passionate outburst of words.

*I shall arise and go now!*

W.B Yeats    Lake Isle of Innisfree

**Metonymy.**    Replacing a thing by some other thing
with which it is actually connected.

*The pen is mightier than the sword.*

**Synecdoche.**  Replacing the whole by a part, or a part by
the whole. A kind of metonymy.

*I live under my own roof.*    ( I live in my own house)

**Hyperbole.**    An exaggeration,  for effect.

*Into the jaws of Death,*
*Into the mouth of Hell*
*Rode the six hundred,*

Alfred Lord.Tennyson, *The Charge of the Light Brigade.*

**Antithesis**      A balance of opposing ideas.

*Better to reign in hell than serve in heaven.*

**Climax** Climax consists in the arranging of several statements in order of ascending importance. Anticlimax is the opposite: the arranging of items so that the last is a sudden descent in importance,

*Who sees with equal eye, as God of all,*
*A hero perish, or a sparrow fall,*

*Atoms or systems into ruin  hurled,*
*And now a bubble burst, and now a world.*

POPE, *Essay* on *Man*

**Euphemism.** The substitution on  an indirect and pleasing expression instead of a direct and harsh one.

*The Prince of Darkness* ( The Devil)
*To pass away* (To die)

# Grammar and Syntax

The most popular poem written today is the prose poem. Yet many writers pay insufficient attention to the rules of grammar, syntax, tense or punctuation all of which are an essential part of prose. Indeed these necessary attributes of prose appear to be low on the list of priorities within the modern educational system. I, hope I will be forgiven for including here a brief resumé of the more fundamental rules of grammar and syntax.

## THE NOUN

The names we give to things are called nouns.
e.g.        *cat, tree, John*

GENDER is a form of the noun used to indicate sex.

In modern English we have adopted what is called natural gender i.e.   gender corresponds to sex. We make nouns denoting male things of the masculine gender, nouns denoting female things of the feminine gender, and nouns denoting dead or lifeless objects of the neuter gender.

## CASE

The relation of a noun to another word in the sentence is called Case. The subject is said to be in the nominative case because it is the chief name word in the sentence,  (*John* is sick) the object complement in the accusative or objective case, ( John struck *Peter* ) and when a noun indicates possession it is said to be in the genitive or possessive case. It's in *Mary's garden.* (Genitive Case)

# SYNTAX

(a) A wo*man was* standing.

(b) The wo*men were* standing.

In (a) woman is nominative to the verb *was standing*; in *(b)* *women* is nominative to *were standing.* In (a) the subject *is* singular, in *(b)* it is plural; so we change the verb in (b) from the singular to the plural. *Was* is said to agree with *woman,* and *were* to agree with *women.* In grammar the agreement or relation of any word with another is governed by the laws of syntax This co-relation of subject-singular verb to singular noun, and plural verb to plural noun is one of the most important laws of syntax.

## ABSTRACT NOUNS

Words that apply to ideas or states of being, that is to notions that only exist in our minds, are called abstract nouns; all other are called concrete nouns.

*Constitution* (abstract) *Forest* (concrete)

## PROPER NOUNS

A noun that applies to only one thing is called a proper noun; a noun that can be applied to many things of its kind is called a common noun.

*Peter* (proper) *Ship* (common)

## COLLECTIVE NOUNS

A Collective noun is a noun that stands for a number of separate objects that are for the moment considered as one thing. e.g. *Committee*

# THE ADJECTIVE

Adjectives are words that qualify, or restrict in meaning, the nouns they accompany.

> (a)    A *large* building.
> *(b)*    Her voice seemed *shallow*

In (a) the adjective *large* is closely joined to the noun *building,* which it qualifies; this is called the epithet use. In (b) the adjective is separated from its noun *voice* by the verb or predicate. This use therefore is called predicative.

> (c) He is *better* than ever.

The adjective *better* qualifies the pronoun *he.* It is used predicatively, as is usually the case with adjectives qualifying pronouns.

## POSSESSIVE ADJECTIVES

The words *my, her, his, its, our, your,* and *their* are called possessive adjectives. They are sometimes regarded as forms of the genitive case of the personal pronouns.

(a)    *Each* hair on her head stood erect.
*(b)*    *Every* hair on her head stood erect.

These sentences illustrate the slight difference in meaning between *each* and *every.*  Each is used to separate the different units more, while *every* is used in a more collective sense.

(a)    They departed, each to their own house
*(b)*    Neither were prepared for their chores.

Common mistakes are exemplified in these sentences. The distributive adjectives are from their meaning singular. *Their* in (a) should be his (or *her),* and *were* in (b) should be *was* and *their* should be *his.*

# COMPARATIVE ADJECTIVES

The comparative degree is a form of the adjective used to express a comparison between two things, the superlative degree is used to compare more than two things.

The use of degrees of comparison is restricted almost entirely to adjectives of quality. *Much* and *little* (adjectives of quantity), *many* and *few* (adjectives of number), are about all the others.

# PRONOUNS

Words that are used in place of nouns are called pronouns. Without pronouns, we would be required to repeat the name of everything - on every occasion we mentioned it.

I. Demonstrative Pronouns: *This, that, these, those, such,*

2. Numeral Pronouns:

(a)  Indefinite: *all, any, any one; both, several, certain; enough, few, many; none, some.*
 *(b)* Definite: *One, two, thirty,* etc.
3  Distributive: *Each, either, neither.*
4  Interrogative: *Who, whose, whom, which, what, whoever.*

# PERSONAL AND POSSESSIVE PRONOUNS

I have lost my watch.

In this sentence "I" is substituted for the name of some person who is not named; it is therefore a pronoun. Such pronouns are called personal pronouns. When a person talks of himself or of those associated with him, he uses the pronouns *I, me, my* or *mine, we, us, ours* or *yours.* These are called first personal pronouns. When he addresses some person or persons directly, be uses the pronouns *you, your,* or *yours.* These are called second personal pronouns.

23

## REFLEXIVE PRONOUNS

### He blamed *himself*

The object of the verb is the pronoun *himself* which clearly refers to the same person as the subject. Such pronouns as this are called reflexive pronouns and compounded of the word self (or *selves)* and various forms of the personal pronouns.

## RELATIVE PRONOUNS

### Those *who* have had their clothes stolen can re-enter.

Who in this sentence is evidently a pronoun, for it refers to some persons. It does more: it helps to introduce a group of words that tells us something about the persons *Who,* in performing this double duty-referring back to some noun or pronoun and carrying on the statement regarding this noun or pronoun-is called a relative pronoun. *Those* is said to be its antecedent. In nearly every case a relative pronoun has an antecedent, usually a noun or pronoun, but sometimes a whole sentence, to which it is closely related.

## THE VERB

Verbs used transitively and intransitively.

(a)  He gave ten pounds for the new wood.
(b)  The new wood *gave off* a pleasant smell.
(c)  On the slightest pressure, the new wood gave.

In the three sentences above the word *gave* expresses the action, and we call it a verb. In each of the examples, however, the verb has a different meaning. In (a) it means handed *over* (or some such similar meaning). When we are told he handed over, we at once expect to be told what he handed over; the sense is not complete, and we transfer our attention from the verb to the object that is acted upon by the verb. Verbs that carry on the attention in this way are said to be used transitively, and the thing to which the attention is transferred is called the object. The object is in the objective (or accusative) case. In (a) the object is *pounds.* The word that stands for the person that does the action -he in this case is called the subject, in the nominative case; and the rest of the sentence is called the predicate. In (b) the new wood does not give a smell in the active sense that the man gave the pounds. The sense of the single word *gave* is less complete. The verb, indeed, requires the assistance of another word, *off,* to give it a transitive force. *Gave* in *(c)* concludes the sense; the mind of the reader is satisfied, and is not carried on to some object. The verb in this case is used intransitively. A verb is transitive when the action passes over from the doer of the action to something else; it is intransitive when the action stops with the verb.

## THE MOOD OF A VERB

The mood of a verb is the form it takes to show the kind of state or action it represents.

Examples.

(a) I *go* to France in the morning..
(b) *Go* to bed immediately.
(c) Let me *go.*
(d) I am ready to *go* at a minute's notice.
(e) He bought the business as a *going* concern.
(f) *Going* is hard to bear.

In all these sentences the verb has a similar meaning, but to some extent a difference exists. In (a) the speaker states a fact; in (b) he expresses a command or entreaty; in (c) he begs or commands some one to permit him to go; in (d) *to go* is used apart from the speaker: the actual going is not made

25

the outstanding action on the part of the speaker; in (e) *going* is used as an adjective; in (f) it is used as a noun. The difference in meaning lies in the mood or intention of the subject. Thus verbs can reflect the mood of their subject. In (a) we have the indicative or declarative; in (b) the imperative; in *(c)* and (d) the infinitive (without a subject) ; in *(e)* we have what is called a participle; and in (f) a gerund.

Subjunctive Mood.

In the subjunctive mood, the attitude of the speaker is that of a wish or desire. Verbs that reflect such a mood are said to be in the subjunctive. Doubt and hesitation are common in this mood. The subjunctive is found chiefly in sentences containing the word *if.* These are called hypothetical sentences, because they express a suggestion or hypothesis.

> *If I were you, If it were true, If you please.*

*You* is not the subject of *please.* The sentence means, ' If it *Please* you.' Please is subjunctive, agreeing with *if.* Since they express desire, condition or determination, the present and past tenses of the subjunctive mood carry a suggestion of the future tense as well. For example, *God save the King* expresses a hope that God *will* save the King.

Imperative Mood.

|  |  |
|---|---|
| (a) | *Don't do* it. |
| *(b)* | *Let's go.* |
| (c) | *You go.* |

This verb expresses a command or entreaty. In (a) we have the command put negatively. In *(b)* it is put more as an entreaty. The subject of the imperative *(you)* is generally omitted, except in the emphatic form (c).

## Infinitive Mood.

This mood of the verb is used with no subject. It therefore has no number or person. The infinitive mood can usually be recognised by the word *to* actually appearing or understood.

(a)  I mean *to leave.*
*(b)  To fight* is your only hope.
(c)  All you do is  *complain..*

## TENSE
### Change of Tense.

As a car *approached* a town the driver *blows his*  horn
to let the people know that the car is *coming.*

This is a common mistake. The writer begins in the past tense, and concludes the sentence in the present. The one tense should be retained throughout.  Sometimes a writer, to make his narrative more vivid, drops into the present: this is called the Historic Present. But a change of tense should always be carefully watched.

Strong and Weak Verbs.

Take the verb *write* Its past tense is *wrote* its perfect participle *written.* These three parts are called its principal parts, because all other parts of its  conjugation are derived from them. To form its past tense it changes the root-vowel of the present ;  to form the perfect participle it adds n. A strong verb is one that forms its past and perfect participle by vowel-change; a weak verb adds *d ,ed*  or t to form its past tense.

| *Tense* | *Indefinite* | *Continuous* | *Perfect* |
|---|---|---|---|
| Present | I ask | I *am* asking | I have asked |
| Past | I asked | I was asking | I had asked |
| Future | I shall ask | I shall be asking | I shall have asked |

# THE ADVERB

*(a)*  Who loudly complained.
*(b)*  You now consider yourself
*(c)*   Having spent my latter days here.
*(d)*  How will that be?
*(e)*  Certainly before my life ends I hope
*(f)*  I, however, am better placed.
*(g)*  I had but one trick.
*(h)*  If one is often unsuccessful,
*(i)*  But shortly after this,
*(j)*  He had so presumptuously offered.

In (a) *loudly* tells us how he *complained.* It evidently affects the meaning of the verb *complained.* We say, therefore, that loudly modifies the verb *complained.* Similarly in (b) we have *now* modifying the verb *consider;* and similar uses may be observed in (c), (d), (e), (f) (with regard to *better),* etc. In (f), *however* does not tell us particularly about the verb *am placed.* It refers rather to the whole idea in the sentence : we may say, therefore, that it modifies the whole sentence. But in (g) means *only* i.e. *only one.* Clearly, *but* here modifies the word *one,* which is an adjective. In (i) we read , *shortly after this* Here the adverb affects the meaning of *after this,* which is a prepositional phrase. In (j) *presumptuously* modifies the verb *offered;* but *so* modifies *presumptuously.* Adverbs are words which modify (or restrict in meaning) (i) verbs (their commonest use) ; (ii) adjectives ; (iii) adverbs; (iv) prepositions ; (v) sentences. They relate to verbs as adjectives do to nouns.

Kinds of Adverbs.

*Loudly* tells us the way or the manner in which he complained. It is called, therefore, an adverb of manner. Adverbs of manner usually answer the question, *How? How* did he complain? Answer: loudly. This class of adverb is very numerous. Ther*e are examples in (f) and (j). Now* tells us the time when he might consider himself. It is called, therefore, an adverb of time. It answers the question, *When?* Adverbs of the same kind are *soon, late, afterward, yesterday, to-morrow,* etc. *Here* in (c) tells us the place where he would spend his days. It is therefore an adverb of place, answering the question, *Where?* Similar adverbs are *within, there, above, yonder,* etc. *Often* in *(h)* tells *us* the number of times the action occurred. It is called *an* adverb of number. It answers the question, *How often?* Others are *once, twice,* etc.; *frequently, rarely, seldom,* etc. In *(j) so* tells us how far or to what degree the action was presumptuous. It is called an adverb of degree, answering the question, *How much?* similar adverbs are *very, somewhat, entirely, too,* etc. *But* in (g) is an adverb. of degree. *Certainly* in *(e)* affirms or states a fact positively These adverbs are called adverbs of affirmation or negation.

## CONJUNCTIONS

Conjunctions are words that join single words, phrases, or sentences. Conjunctions that simply join ideas together, like *and* and *but,* are called co-ordinating conjunctions. Conjunctions that join one idea to another, and make one idea explain or restrict the other, are called subordinating conjunctions. They make one idea subordinate that is, a servant to the other. Common co-ordinating conjunctions are (a) *but, still, yet, however:* these express contrast; *(b) and, both,* expressing additions; (c) *either . . . Or, Or,* expressing choice; (d) *therefore,* for, etc., expressing cause or effect. There are several classes of subordinating conjunctions; they are named according to their uses; e.g. *when* expresses time, *where* place, *because* reason, etc. It should be noted that a subordinating conjunction introduces a subordinate clause,

Groups of words like *in order that, in case,* are described as compound conjunctions.

## THE PREPOSITION

A word that is used to show the relation between a noun or pronoun and another word in the same sentence is called a preposition. Prepositions are said to govern nouns or pronouns and are usually placed in front of the word or words that they govern.

Examples;

*at, near, above, about, to, over, under, on, in, inside, outside, after, before, with, from* etc. Phrases such as *on behalf of, as to, with regard to* constitute compound prepositions.

Other Uses of Prepositions.

Prepositions are used in all manner of ways. After verbs we have such prepositions as differ *from*, prevail *on,* labour *at,* etc. After nouns, see a match *for,* a stain *on,* etc. We can have prepositions after adjectives and adverbs, e.g. different *from,* inferior *to,* regardless *of,* independently *of* simultaneously *with,* etc.


## SYNONYMS


Words like *talker* and *speaker,* that resemble each other closely in meaning are called *synonyms.* Synonyms sometimes are a little different in meaning like the two we have given. Sometimes, like *often* and *frequently,* - *happen* and *occur,* there is hardly any difference.

# THE SENTENCE

Every sentence can be divided into two parts, the subject and the predicate. The subject is the word or group of words which denotes the person or thing of which the predicate is said. The predicate is all that is said of the person or thing denoted by the subject.

# CLAUSES

Clauses are parts of a sentence that each contain a predication. The number of finite verbs in a sentence gives the number of clauses. The habit of joining simple sentences with *and* is very common both in speech and in writing. It is natural to do so but in time it becomes as boring as the over use of simple sentences. A sentence that contains one main predication is called a simple sentence; one main predication and one or more subordinate predications is called a complex sentence.

## INDEPENDENT AND DEPENDENT CLAUSES

A main clause is sometimes called an independent clause. As the name indicates, this is a clause which can stand alone and is not dependent on another clause:

The water got deeper and the people cried.

The above sentence has two independent or main clauses joined by *and.*

If we change it to read:

*When the water got deeper* the people cried.

we still have two clauses, but the first clause has now become dependent on the second, or subordinate to it.

Subordinate Clauses

As we have seen, a subordinate clause is dependent on another clause, the main clause. There are four types of subordinate clause, depending on their position or function in relation to the main clause:

- nominal or noun clauses
- adverbial clauses
- relative clauses
- comparative clauses

Nominal clauses

These are subordinate clauses with a function in the sentence similar to that of the noun phrase. They can act as the subject, object, or complement of the main clause.

Adverbial clause

These are subordinate clauses with a function in the sentence adverbial:. Thus they modify the main clause by adding information about time, location, concession, cause, etc. They are usually linked to the main clause by a conjunction. They can occur in most parts of a sentence:

> She must phone home *if she is lost.*
> *If she is lost* she must phone home.

Relative Clause

These are subordinate clauses with an 'adjectival' function in the sentence, as modifiers of a noun phrase:

> The house *which I bought* was detached.

In this sentence the relative clause is joined to the main clause by the relative pronoun *which.* It refers back to the noun phrase *the house* which is called the antecedent of the relative clause.

Comparative Clauses

These are subordinate clauses which modify comparative
adverbs and adjectives. The main comparative adjectives are
the ones with regular *-er* endings - *older, fatter, harder,*
simpler, etc. Other comparative words are *more, less, better,*
*worse,* etc.

e.g. *It was harder* than I thought.


Restrictive Clauses.

These are relative clauses in which punctuation plays a
crucial part.

> My brother who lives in England is sick.
> My brother, who lives in England, is sick.

In the first sentence, the relative clause *who lives in England*
is restrictive, specifying which brother. The speaker thus
perceives a certain emphasis in the first sentence: My brother
who lives in *England.* . . Not the one who lives in *France.* In
the second sentence, the relative clause, which has been
marked off in commas, is not restrictive. The information
between the commas is not restricted, and the sentence has
two things to say: (a) the speaker has a brother who is sick
(b) that brother happens to live in England. Punctuation thus
conveys the information that the speaker in the first sentence
has more than one brother while the speaker in the second
sentence has only one brother, and that brother lives in
England.

# Some Observations on Modern Poetry

1. A poem is not a short story.

2. Economy of language is the chief discipline.

3. Similes and Metaphor are considered naive.

4. Figures of speech are rarely used.

5. Stress patterns and the natural rhythms of speech are still employed as disciplines by many poets.

6. Everyday language is used to understate the ideas in a poem and to disarm the reader.

7. Bombast, Rhetoric and Moralising are avoided.

8. The "colour" and "texture" of words and their emotional stimulus are the main preoccupation of poets in their efforts to capture the abstract.

9. Poems gain by what is omitted.

10. Suitable topics are dictated by fashion.

Beyond this it's impossible to set out rules where there are no rules and every writer has the freedom to set their own.

# *Modern Poetry.*

What then has all this to do with the way poetry is written today. When practising music, students often use a metronome to help them establish a regular sense of time. By practising the piece over and over again they make themselves familiar with the changing rhythms of the piece. However, once they feel confident with the piece they switch off the metronome and allow the human touch and their own personality to shine through. In recent years matters of rhythm and metre have been almost totally ignored in poetry; yet non-metric poetry could never have existed if metric poetry had not existed first. The whole concept of non-metric would have no meaning unless people had formerly known what metric meant. In the same way the avoidance of alliteration and rhyme only makes sense if people have an understanding of what is being avoided. Most poems in English even today, contain some form of rhythm. Rhythm in this sense is a of combination of both similarity and difference. It is used in modern poetry to draw words with similar syllables together and not necessarily at the ends of lines. One is not concerned with rhyme here, more with assonance and this is one of the ingredients still regularly used in modern poetry. The combination of opposing ideas such as *fast* and *slow*, or *dark* and *light* within a poem is also still a central feature of even the most avant-garde poetry. Indeed the *sound* of a poem has always been its central magic. At one time all poetry was intended to be recited  aloud and to an audience. The majority of people were unable to read, and anyway books were too expensive. The habit of reading poetry silently to oneself only arose with the widespread availability of books. Today poetry is divided into that which is intended for performance in front of a live audience and that which works better on the printed page; and yet, the importance of the sounds in a poem should never be overlooked.

# The Poet as Ikat Weaver

With wool and string
and a backstrap loom
she gives them cloth.

It folds without breaking,
on the body feels
like second skin. Magical

her hand on the shuttle,
taking weft through warp,
reveals the pattern,

already in the treads.
They call her goddess,
know nothing of the nights

in prayer and fasting,
the suffrage to the spirits
of those gone before,

a life spent learning
the complicated turns
of message strings, ikat

knots that repel evil
from the tiedyed bespoke
stuff of her own soul.


*Aine Miller*                    *Dublin*

This poem employs a  technique called enjambment whereby
the poet breaks lines so that the last line or last word of the
last line in a stanza is connected grammatically to the first

line in the next stanza. To work correctly, the word or line which is enjambed thus must be capable of being included in either stanza but secures extra meaning using this technique For example as above:

| | |
|---|---|
| her hand on the shuttle,<br>taking weft through warp,<br>reveals the pattern, | This stanza makes perfect sense |
| already in the treads. | without this line |

so that a sense of more is achieved using this technique.

The use of this technique in a poem about weaving is particularly appropriate because there is something of enjambment in the art of weaving Ikat weaving is a practice in Malaysia. It takes weavers a lifetime to learn to tie ikat knots. It is necessary to conceive the pattern *in toto* before tying and weaving begins. The tying of knots has supernatural significance in eastern religions. The poet sees an obvious parallel between this weaving and the work of poem-making. The moment of insight or vision seems to be already there just waiting for the poet to create the right vessel to contain it. Like wise the learning of the craft of poem-making is a lifetime occupation for the poet as it is for the weaver.

# All Souls

In that November place I stood beside worn stone.
As carved names faded with the light, memories
paled too, or hid behind my guilty heart.
Rain threatened but held off.

Then traveller girls, two of them,
struggled up the path. Barelegged,
sturdy, they brought red plastic buckets
spilling sudsy tears.

Two magdalens, armed with chamois cloths
and sprays, gibed each other.
Gave me the bold eye.
I watched them hitch skirts inside their knickers
to shiny up their father's tombstone,
(a statue of the virgin)

anoint away all earthly trespass
with Ajax and a scrubbing brush.

*Eileen Casey*                              *Tallaght*


This poem derives its success from an affectionate
contrast between its sacred setting, a graveyard on the
*"Feast of The Holy Souls"* and the vivacity of young
girls and their activities. This contrast is carried on into
the objects in the poem, *carved names, tombstone,
statue of the virgin* as compared with *red plastic
buckets, knickers, Ajax* and *a scrubbing brush.*

# Song of the Cidermen

The South Lotts cidermen host
neverend, three to a doorway parties
where old, onceuponasmiles
light up usedtobe stories.
Cartoon rituals of the kissmearse society
as they brush down this season's
VdeP offerings and catwalk into oblivion.
Sadcity sadmen summerdancing
by the jewelshine Liffey,
a menace of Hollywood hoodlum overcoats
and patchwork histories.
Dramatic poses in slipaway sidestreets
offers to tinwhistle your favourite tune
for sixtypee.
Rageroars from the chaoschorus
"Gwanhomes "and " Gedoutaheres",
the Gregorian chant of the midnightmen
from nowhere.
Neon green shines peppermint
on the rainblack road
we drive by, smug, safe,
snug in our metalflesh.

*Michael Herron*            *Kildare*

This poem is an excellent example of the use of composite
words. The word *"kissmearse"*    made up of the words
kiss, me, arse, is a single concept condensed into a single
word, an adjective, used to describe a irreverent and
uncaring society. Again the word *"rainblack"* describes
precisely a colour not normally seen in paint catalogues.
Not all of the words in the poem are coined of necessity
however, but this style adds to the charm and atmosphere
of the piece as a whole,

## 'What about now?'

The mist in the bell
Dulls the knell;
Its harsh clang is softer, sweeter,
But still audible -

Just as we paint
Over the taints
Of life -
We approach the end, always
Looking behind.

Life is so sweet and lasts,
But we grasp
It too hard, bite too much;
We crush it into the rotten core
Of the past.

What about now?
We must bow,
Thank Life for each breath she gives us -
   As if it were our last.

*Jude Cosgrove*       *Dublin*


This poem is concerned with healing and time. Time has
been a central concern of poets throughout the ages.    Time
in poetry is basically a philosophical concept. Both
philosophy and psychology are important ingredients in
modern poetry.    The great philosopher Aristotle said

40

*"poetry is more philosophic and of greater significance than history, for its statements are of the nature of universals, whereas those of history are of particulars."*

The unreality of time is a cardinal doctrine of many metaphysical systems and there is a sense in which time is an unimportant characteristic of reality, especially where poetry is concerned.

Henry Vaughan wrote:

> *"I saw eternity the other night*
> *Like a great ring of pure and endless light*
> *All calm, as it was bright;*
> *And round beneath it, Time in hours, days, years*
> *Driven by the spheres."*

Bertrand Russell wrote:

*" Though in thought and in feeling time be real, to realise the unimportance of time is the gate of wisdom. Whoever wishes to see the world truly, to rise above the tyranny of practical desires, must learn to overcome the difference of attitude towards past and future, and to survey the whole stream of time, in one comprehensive vision.*

# Incommunicado

Your body curls
and freezes in pre-birth position
defensive glacial egg
tight as a fossil.

My verbal pickaxe
seeks to grip your polarised denial
words slide off
unable to locate a fissure.

Your back's crystalline curve
spells evasion, and I sit
beyond the frozen circle
of your feigned indifference.

*Eithne Cavanagh*          *Rathmines*


Although this poem deals with an abstract subject, ( i.e. the failure to communicate ) it does so by the use of some very concrete and beautiful images which conjure up vivid pictures in the mind.

# Broken Statues

When you jumped from
the railings, you stood
transfixed, frozen in time,
holding your ludicrous positions,
until simian grimaces
cracked even the most rigid
among your infant ranks:
There among the broken statues,
you laugh at shattered form
until the tears stream
down your impish faces.

The frozen smiles of politicians
commend the power of icons
on pedestals of Church and State:
And I search for cracks again,
with iconoclastic zeal,
to shatter rigid form,
to laugh at broken statues.

*Declan Collinge*                    *Templeogue*

This poem draws a good analogy between behaviour in
childhood and the habits of adult life. The poem suggests
that the innocent play of the children was a portent of
attitudes which would crystallise later. The imagery holds
throughout.

# Someone Big is Dead

My father sent me to the church
　　　　　to find out who was dead.


"There's a huge crowd hanging about
it must be someone big-
　　get down and find out who's dead"

I got there just in time
to see the procession from the church
　　　　　to the hearse outside the gates
bearing in their midst
　　　　　　　　a white coffin.


*Liam O'Meara*　　　　　　　　*Dublin*


This poem derives its success from the element of surprise coupled with the coded information in the term "a white coffin" meaning a child's coffin. The poem is carefully crafted, building up to a suspense, capitalising on such incidents as occur in everyday life but which are by their very nature *poetic*.

# Lug Worm Morning

Under an October sky
we waited for colour's decision,
he the ageing father and me the boy.

Sand was our planet
soft, wet, the sea's revision
with wellingtoned feet on it.

Bent over, he sieved the sand
half seeing the squirming limbless
energetic and aquatic in his hand.

When the bucket was full
the sea came swimming in
my memory,
cold handle, webbed gull,
the *Connaught spit,* the him.

*James Conway*                    *Rathgar.*


This poem is a reverie about the poets father. It derives its
power from the directness of the first lines, e.g. *Sand was
our planet -When the bucket was full.* The sparse description
of the recollections enhance their accuracy and add strength
to the poem's veracity.

# Don't bury me in anything
# I wouldn't be seen dead in.

Shroud me in satin,
white mist, clouds
air brushed, violet
evenings, hyacinth
blue of bells blending
moss softened greens
and yellow
prim yellow roses
in the sunset's warm orange
And gather me amber
and rubies and garnets red
to garland my black birth
when darkness swathes me
in every colour known
and I slip into colours
never even dreamed of.

*Christine Broe      Rathgar*

What appears on first sight to be a poem based on a cliché,
*"I wouldn't be seen dead in  it"* turns out to be a beautiful
piece of work  about colour. The poet envisions death as a
*black birth* and is anxious to take as many colours as
possible from this world with her when she departs. The skill
here is to include a wide range of colours without turning the
poem  simply into a list which is a common fault in modern
poetry.

# Paradise Lost

Through amputated streets
Gabriel takes a short cut
shows me the star-spangled
way to Springburn Station
somewhere out there on
the Siberian Steppes.

Perfection
in the luminous face of
a sleeping child.

In the yellow twilight
a student reads
"Paradise Lost"

The late train sidles in,
We continue our journey
to the Cherry Orchard.

*Daphne Kirkpatrick*                    *Cornwall*

# They Think I'm Mad

When the heavens opened
mother held an umbrella
over the table. Occasionally
drops of rain made their way
into my cereal. Plink. Plink. Fizz.
Like in the Ad. for Disprin.
We kept a ready supply - she said
the small pink ones were mine.
One night I sucked an entire bottle,
their taste against my palate
like a hundred penny sherbets.
When I didn't wake for school
it never occurred to her to dash
out to the phone, or bundle me up
and leg it down to the taxi rank.

*Celia de Fréine*                    *Ranelagh*

In this piece the poet marvels at the simplicity of rearing children in her mother's time, when choices were few and parents were under less stress.

# In Bewley's, Saturday 9.15 am.

Christ passes by the hovel of my heart.
Post Christian morality emerges as my new Saviour.
When nothing is wrong everything is right.
Where nobody  sins, everybody does
what they want to do.
As to a beautiful woman,  I am dead.
Hanging around here like a wet mass.
I am biochemically sound, so I am healthy
and could not be depressed when one considers
the balance of my high drug intake.
I am swarming in the essential saviour of my heart,
medical drugs and the <u>Like.</u>
I am now living on the optimum of prescribed drugs,
The balance Is just correct!
I have become complete and total.
When it comes to women I haven't a clue.
I'm fifteen and a half stone in weight.
I don't doubt my existence, I don't shout look at  me
and at the same time hear myself saying
"look at me."
I have feeble social abilities, the more beautiful the
young lady is, the more helpless I become. Why do I
sit here and bemoan and hope. My values, in a way
are governed by fickle tastes and instincts where the
pleasure principle is paramount. I know what I will do,
I will be.
Inhale a passive complacency and live my life as a
mediocrity of failure, being polite to everybody.
My internal furnacewill ebb and flow
breakdown and be built up.

*Andrew Carr*                    *Phibsboro*

In this piece the poet is taking stock of his situation. It is
remarkably honest and self revealing. By this means the poet
establishes an empathy with the reader, who is likewise
inspired to look behind the mask of everyday living. The
poem is also remarkable for the regular use of interjections.

# Black Mantilla

Close to the chief mourners
She accepts whispered words
Dabbing her eyes
With the back of a gloved hand

She turned up
With black mantilla
Tear stained weathered face.

Who is she?
Winks, elbows
The family wonder.
Invite her home to share their meal.

Ash dropping from ruby lips
A half glass of  Paddy
She checks the daily paper
Wanders on
To the next funeral.

*Stella Hayes*                    *Rathfarnham*

Nicely observed, an unusual theme with a humorous
treatment. Humour as used here does nothing to undermine
the seriousness of the work.

# The Spring Clean

That one room you tackled
before any of the others
(which were less of a challenge)
became the room through which
you gained your strength
and measured all tasks.
That room stretched your capacity
widened the four walls of your perception
drew an energy up from a well
deep within the earth's eternal source.
That one room is your testimony
to a truth you will not lose:
after this room, all else is easy.
Now moving from room to room
you are connected to a whole,
assured of an ethical space.
A certain place
orchestrating a dream
full of sweet idle moments.

*Noelle Vial*                    *Killybegs*

# Cobwebs

Sweeps on hedges

Filigree trees

Jacob's ladders
Tempting the breeze.

Spun with gossamer
Beaded with dew
Art and artifice
And laceyness too

*Ita Kenny*                    *Churchtown*

51

# Kiritimati Island

Her young body excited you
with dreams of dancing all night
bodies locked in lovemaking.

So you put me ashore with my trunk
and my child
Left us in a place
where natives ride donkeys
sleep in mud huts.

Your cargo of gold and cut stones sold
You are again the country squire
at ease with the hunt
Time now to browse through your library.

The nursery redundant
My locket,  proof we were lost at sea.

Your freedom guaranteed
by  my silence.

*Mary Maguire*                              *Terenure.*


# How Could You?

You leave
I'm lost
Memories flood my mind
With you
goes the me I became
being with you.

*Phyllis McGuirk*                              *Inchicore*

# Neighbours

We shared a canopy
the first number of strokes
 before taking on the hazards
 of respective ladders

I was putting brown
over cream emulsion paint
while Freddie next door
pocketing a rag passed through the window
                              by his missis
 put cream- the same shade of cream
                     over brown

We stopped a moment
-dipped brushes

I remember Freddie's face
and I'm sure he remembers mine.


*Liam O'Meara*                    *Inchicore*


The circumstances described in this poem are ironic. Irony is where the unexpected occurs, sometimes with unhappy consequences and yet causes us to smile. In this poem the characters are not only rubbing each other out (decoratively) but, even though they are next door neighbours, they hardly know each other.

# The Speech before Words

Your first language was Chinese
learnt from an amah
while your parents were talking
to a colonial world.

Your grandfather forbade you to speak it;
and like a late frost, an English
boarding school deflowered
the fertile blossom of your tongue.

And now, you cannot remember
even your first
stammering words, the Chinese
for ma-ma, da-da.

They have taken away the language
of your innocence,
but they cannot destroy
the speech before words.

Your tongue paints
hieroglyphics on my chest
writing poems
in the silence of love.

*Jeremy Young*                    *Rathgar*

54

# Afterbloom

A slipper of bleached rose blossom
glazed the wet pavement
outside your window.

Your only legacy, reminder
that you once reeked of Royalty
and old world charm.

Smacked of golden dawns
and crimson sunsets
Poised,
immaculate in emulsion colours.

A handful of limp petals
left behind on the dank tarmac
your final will and testament.

*Tommy Murray*          *Co. Meath*

This is a poem saying goodbye to someone recently departed.
Poems on this topic are normally dour and depressing but
this poem is uplifting and gives a general feeling of lightness
and beauty - without sentimentality.

# Near Nirvana

My Glory-hole was pungent
with unctuous putty
Paintbrushes softened in turpentine
in cups that had no handles.

Timber toolboxes hosted plumb-hobs
and spirit-levels with grape-green
molten jewels sloshing around their bellies.

A boot-last and tins of tacks
crazed plates and dusty overalls.
Cobweb-swagged corners
graced this cornucopia of clutter.

Here it was I'd sit alone,
Coaxing glissando from an old gappy comb.
while I licked my wounds
or warmed to my secrets.

Yet I've never felt myself,
in landscape, seascape. skyscape
cloister or oratory,
more firmamental,
than there in that womb-dark recess
under the grumbling stairs.

*Maureen McAteer*            *Gweedore*

The poet says that she has never has felt as "firmamental"
in landscape, seascape or skyscape as she does in the dark
recess under the stairs. This is the opposite to what people
expect to read in a poem. True poets see things differently!

# Victory Day

In London town
They celebrate victory
With doves
And laser beams,
And the queen mother
Smiles at Spitfires
Flying overhead
And remembers the bombs
Dropping on Dresden
On Nagasaki
On Hiroshima
And sheds a little tear
Just a little tear,
To honour the holy dead.

*Denis Collins*         *Wexford*


# Temper

Latent
in a mass of memory
are ice words
that in expression
slush

While anger
which refused to boil
is left compressed
and frozen.

*Eithne Hogan*         *Clondalkin*

# Regrowth

My nail's grown again
the pinkie snapped that night
our last together
so painfully
cracked, midway down
but didn't bleed
I felt the throb despite absorption
robbing our passion
when I noticed the pain.

Yet it's healed now
imperceptibly- not like
when  it broke
quietly without fuss
It mended, the way small things do
but the big things, like repairing ripped hearts
how much time will it take
to heal mine?

*Alice McEvoy*                    *Belfast*

# Shadowless

Uneasy in the vortex
searching for something
I know is there-
I feel it in the windsweep
bending grass heads,
rising in the heat haze
over viridian plains
and when the mist
makes strange shapes
of lavender gorse,
it moves down the mountain,
shadowless in its passing,

*Phil McCloskey*                    *Donegal*

58

# Slieve Blooms

Near your feet
we each absorbed the other
a mother's presence
grounding me.
Now distanced, fleeting glimpses
of your womanly curves
excite me to observe
your more intimate moments.
Early morning,
lifting your navy nightshade
woman child,
you lay bare in startling clarity
such beauty, etched in fine detail.
Times,
your contours hide in veils of mist
where sight of you remains an act of faith.
On azure days from Cashel Rock
your bosom beautiful
speaks a universality of seasonal tongues
nurturing a need of place and past.
Constant as the Northern Star
you are ever on my horizon.

*Elsie Deevey*                    *Portlaoise*


The Slieve Blooms are a range of mountains in the south of
Ireland. The poet addresses the mountains as if they were a
woman, and not just any woman, but her mother. As the
poem progresses it becomes clear that the poet is at once
addressing both the mountains and her mother.

# A Benediction

When he was dressed
and sitting in his chair
I knelt before him
put on his warm lined boots
lifted each helpless leg
placed each foot
on the wheelchair step
his hand on my head
a benediction.

*Breda Sullivan*                    *Westmeath*

# Token of Love

Mother's day,
the opportunity
to honour mothers
for their mothering.

My children
went to town
came home
with big smiles
and a bunch
of tired tulips
yawning in cellophane.

*June Murphy*                    *Longford*

Two poems about love given, and love returned.

# You Win Again

You threw the Knife

onto the table

where I'd just

poured out my heart.

Then you twisted it

before putting it away

for the next time.


*Ann Comerford*            *Wexford*


This excellent poem is remarkable because it contains only
one adjective. Too many adjectives undermine poetry and
bleed nouns, of their power.

# St. Kevin

After early morning chorus
and love's twist and flutter
she flew to where he was kneeling
stiffened like a fakir
raising rigid arms

Towards his God who hovered
unseen above the bronze
of the sprouting young oak branches;
she rustled to fit grasses
between his chilled fingers;
then round eyed, straight tailed
settled in his hands.
Inflated charcoal feathers
covered eggs blue and freckled;
in rain and broken sunshine
a warmth of supplication
helped the incubation
until his sinner's palms
Moved to screams of goosefleshed
orange throated fledglings.
He prayed while she reared them
*Laudamus te Deum*

*Gillian Somerville-Large*     *Kilkenny*

This poem describes a subject who lived many hundreds of
years ago. It is successful because it avoids the use of any
modern imagery  but concentrates on the elemental and the
sacred and uses words appropriate to the subject. *(fakir)*

# Getting There

I keep my smile wide
for other people's milestones.
Ensure I have in easy reach
the necessary oohs and ahs
to greet the latest news of who's just got together,
coupled and/or multiplied.
And practice an appreciative grin
(no hint of jealousy) for the latest
 corporate victory of a friend

It may be choice or default
 that pushed me towards
 the secondary roads.
 I didn't have the heart,
(more like the skill)
to navigate the crowded lanes
or join those impatient on the side,
all anxiously awaiting openings.

I'll make my own way.
And though I still don't know
the destination, I'll go
 a slow and crooked path,
 and pray I like the view
 on getting there.

*Nessa O'Mahony*                    *Rathfarnham*

In this piece the poet is taking stock of her situation. It is
remarkably honest and self revealing. By this means the poet
establishes an empathy with the reader, who is likewise
inspired to look behind the mask of everyday living. The
uninhibited theme is complemented by an uninhibited style.

# Land of Stone

In this land of stone
daylight lingers
and when darkness falls,
and lights go out on Mullaghmore,
the stone is luminous still-
ledges of limestone rock,
pocked by centuries
of slow-dripping rain
gashed into grikes and clefts,
in whose narrow chambers,
tiny flowers  flourish - an eruption
of brilliant blues, pinks, purples, yellows
to compensate for all the greyness
Storm - winds drive inland,
from the wild Atlantic
sweeping over the solitariness,
of this charmed place,
twisting the scanty trees
into stunted fantastic shapes
No need for man to analyse
the strange explosion of stone,
or desecrate this wilderness,
Sacred to the Gods - this lunar creation
conceived in the womb of time

*Vera Hughes*                    *Westmeath*

This poem maintains same imagery throughout and successfully establishes that sense of permanence which is promised in the title.

# Awake, Already

*(For Vanessa)*

Awake, already you trust
An arm's length
Outside the blankets, taking a stretch
As the wool pulls
Away. My bare feet leave
Tired, invisible
Prints on the tiles; impossibly blue
The pool soaks
In the air, thin ripples
Feathering an absence
Of birds.

You'll draw the curtain back
On this, on sleeping
New volcanoes to the south
That look on you
Untroubled at the window;
As you are before you
Wound the water's calm
Remorseless face: just before you
Float
To the outside
Of your depth.

*Enda Coyle-Greene*                    *Skerries*

The line breaks in this poem are particularly important
because they constantly allow for a second meaning to be
drawn from the words used.
    Also note the spelling of the word *trust*.

# Blue Denim Boy

They sit crumpled on the bench;
the boy stands uneasily in front,
takes the green bottle
of cheap sherry.
Neat haircut, clean pink face,
shiny silver earring.
He and they:
a lifetime apart
but the distance is shrinking.

*Anne Mac Darby*      *Cill Chainnigh*

# Rage

Rage
starts with a stone in my shoe
a nettle sting of old frustrations.
It's like a dervish
 whirling up into my brain
 flashing incoherent pain
drowning the drudgery of daily decency.

It's like
a powerful drug
that makes me want to take
the stopper out of that quartz crystal
bottle, where a brutal genie,
storm trooper of my soul
 sits sharpening my tongue
· to a fixed bayonet.

*Patrica Anne Moore*          *Co. Clare*

# The Smart Missile

the smart missile sailed
down the chimney
of the house
of the General
of the extreme fascist regime
and that was the end of him

the US commander
appeared on the scene
lopped off the head -
of the dead wolf
and wouldn't you know it
out popped granny

after granny
after granny
after granny
and all of the citizens
unscathed

and now I think it's time
to go to sleep

*Liam O'Meara*                    *Inchicore*

In this piece the poet employs sarcasm to counter the propaganda of the superpowers who promote the idea that modern war can be prosecuted using "surgical strikes" and "clinical accuracy " thereby avoiding civilian casualties. By adopting the mode of a children's fairy tale the poet further undermines the credibility of such suggestions.

# Casualty

Bus stop people
stared in sadness
at a dead cat.

Gingerly juggernauts
swung around
cars slowed down
seventy sixes crept past
our thirty-nine went over
without touching him.

Such a clean cat
and fat
snow-crested chest,
three white paws.

Boarding the bus
one last look

That's my cat !


*Ann Sempers*                 *Palmerstown*

# Sliding Stones

Beyond the gap in the tree
leaves pattern a form

of a faraway house.
 I listen by the quarry

where stones dance
 their shale music.

You stand at the door
I warm to your core.

Stones slide and settle
 when we are together

and mesh one leaf's moment
 in the curtain of our chasm.

*Ann Egan*                    *Co. Kildare*


In this piece the poet draws a parallel between the  power
and monumental forces normally employed in a quarry and
the mutual attraction that exists between herself and the
subject. However, while the intention is to stress the
inevitability of  the convergence, not all of  the imagery is
robust and harsh as evidenced by  " *dance their shale
music*" and  *"one leaf's moment."*

# Intermittent Sound

His watery blue eyes
Follow faces
Lip movements

His hand cupped behind his ear
He listens
Strings sentences
Words
Meaning

Voices lifted
Above conversation pitch
Slump into whispers

He hears perfectly.

*Anne Dean*                                    *Foxrock*

# Exclusion Zone

The dust that settled down to rest
on tree and roof and grass
when Hell's mouth belched
unsettled you, and set you to turn
from all that lay at rest under dust-
Sony Walkman, Mountain Bike
typewriter, poems, guitar,
bed, hearth and door.
However restless now, know
that to turn again would be
to turn to salt or worse.
Walk on, leave all the rest
to dust, take nothing forth
except your life, your life, your life.

*Michael Durack*                              *Co. Clare*

# Expulsion from Paradise

The bronze gates of Eden
slammed against them,
they flee into humanity's first night;
Adam and Eve, expelled from Paradise.

Adam weeps, cowering in shame, but she
shivers with joy under the unmapped stars
her mind pregnant with hope, as if she
knew

of their ordained adventure:
the islands and the oceans they will name,
the making of new cities and mythologies

a new world of their own, wild
to be imagined into being, and tomorrow
the first day of history.

*Liam Aungier*                    *Kildare*

# Lunch Out

A treat. Lunch out
in quite surroundings.
Hunger  rumbles
in the pit of my stomach.

Tinfoil parcel on my plate.
Noisy scrunch to reveal contents
On colourful vegetable bed,
pleading, glassy fish eyes

stare up at my conscience.

*Maria Wallace*                    *Fortunestown*

# Soldier

Laden heavy to your knees
with defeat
you surrender
almost naked to your torn
sandals, the sand
straining between your toes
against what's left
of  your manhood.
An awful sadness
squelching out of what was pure  belief
in your apple eye
now turns bad in your stomach.
Your heart leapt
in the captor's hand
strangely it didn't die.
With lips quivering
trapped words
thick in the throat
are choked.
Swelling up on the tongue
they burst like balloons.

*Marian Finan Hewitt*        *Tallaght*


People sometimes refer to slices of toast as soldiers. This is
not what the poet has in mind, but there are many different
kinds of soldier and so this poem is open to interpretation in
several different contexts.

# In the Library

Every Morning
they ask me
"did you do the back-up"
And every time
I hear the words
back-up
the street at home
floats before my eyes,
my Father
tackling the horse,
moving him under
the shafts of the cart
coaxing him
back-up back-up.

*Mary Guckian*                    *Ringsend*

# Marking Time

You observe how much more light
comes through the glass door,
the double-glazed window
in our modernised sitting-room.
Long overdue, you say,
how long have we been here?
I begin the slow count backwards,
but you are a step ahead,
you pinch the dead leaves from the ivy.
the dry stems twist awkwardly
over the mantelpiece
like an ageing dancer's limbs.
I need to draw the curtains,
stand with my back against the door
before you open your fingers
and examine me, in this harsh light.

*Mary Rose Callan*                    *Dublin*

# Peter and Paula

And in  evening  gown   barely  wrapt
you   don't   get   time  to  think   the
book  being  launched  will    make an
instant   impact  on   its  way  to  some
bargain     basement      shelves     waste
disposal    skips    relations     friends
A speech  by   the    publisher  stressed
tearproof    mascara   being    essential
for  poets  without   a  body  of  work
behind  them    seeking   state    grants
potluck  applications   to   be    writers
in   residence  in   zoos  funeral  parlours
Bowing before applause encore! handing
us    over   to   Manna  Showers  of   no
fixed abode almost  everyone on  the floor
*Sean Carey*                    *Dublin*

At the forefront of modern poetry there are a group of writers described as *" post language poets."* The idea here is that individual words, or groups of words within a poem have their own integrity. Words are used like the brush strokes of a painter, adding to the whole, but not necessarily in chronological or even in a logical order. Images are laid adjacent to one another giving an aggregate picture as in a mosaic, yet each image retains its own perspective.

# Index of poets

Aungier, Liam, *Expulsion from Paradise,* P71 Native of Co Kildare, published in Riposte, Irish Times and Poetry Ireland review.

Broe, Christine *Don't bury me in anything I wouldn't be seen Dead In.* P 46    Lives in Rathgar,   winner of    several    poetry    awards, including 2nd prize in Riposte 1996, 2nd prize in Grand Slam '98 published in Extended Wings, Incognito, Women's Works, Riposte.

Callan, Mary Rose    *Marking Time* P73 lives in Dublin, member of Resonance Writers' Group, Stillorgan. Won  1st Prize in Cork Literary review 1998, also OKI Literary award and 2nd prize in Jonathon Swift Competition. Published., Riposte, Women's Work  & Waterford Review.

Carey, Sean    *Peter and Paula*  P 74, lives in Dublin, has had work published in Britain and USA,   former moderator of *Voice Free.*

Carr, Andrew *Saturday Morning in Bewley's,*P49 lives in Phibsboro, widely published, has had recourse to psychiatric services over 25 years.

Casey, Eileen   *All Souls* P38, lives in Dublin, winner of The Moore Medalion & prizes in Syllables, Hopkins, Boyle Arts Festival, The Scottish International, published in anthologies in Ireland and America.

Cavanagh, Eithne *Incommunicado* P42, lives in Rathmines, native of Co. Wicklow,   winner of Boyle Arts Festival Competition, joint winner of Riposte Competition 1998, has also won prizes in Syllables and Jonathon Swift.   Published in Riposte, Extended Wings, and in several anthologies in Ireland, England and America.

Collinge, Declan, *Broken Statues,* P43, lives in Dublin, has published two books of poetry in English, Fearful Symmetry and Common Ground, and a volume of poems in Irish,  Sealgaireacht. Lectures on Anglo-Irish Literature in Maynooth and much of his work has been broadcast on RTE.

Collins, Denis *Victory Day,* P57, lives in Co. Wexford, artistic director of Wexford Arts Centre, a partner in *"The Works"* publishing group, won prizes in the Scottish International and Syllables, widely published.

Comerford, Ann *You Win Again* P61, lives in Co. Wexford. Widely published. Won the Scottish International Poetry Competition twice, in 1994 and 1996. Member of the Wexford Writers' Group.

Conway, James *Lug Worm Morning* P45, lives in Rathgar, founder of Rathmines Writers' Workshop, won prizes in Syllables Poetry Competition, published Connaught Tribune, Riposte, New Writers, Extended Wings and several other anthologies.

Cosgrove, Jude, *What about Now?,* P40, lives in Dublin published in Riposte and several other periodicals.

Coyle-Greene, Enda *Awake Already* P65, lives in Co. Dublin, published in Incognito, Podium 2, Asylum and Riposte. Winner of Cootehill Award 1995, The Jonathon Swift Award 1997. Took part in *The Poetry Ireland Review* Introductions 1998.

De Fréine, Celia *They Think I'm Mad,* P48, poet, critic, and screenwriter, also writes in Irish, awarded Arts Council Bursary in Literature, widely published.

Dean, Anne *Intermittent Sound* P70, lives in Dublin, has been writing for eight years, has won prizes in Clonmel, Ballyshannon and Listowel, published in Poetry Ireland, Women's Work, Acorn, Extended Wings and Riposte.

Deevey, Elsie *Slieve Blooms,* P59, lives in Port Laoise, a descendant of the McHugh Clan who settled on the Slieve Bloom Mountains after the Battle of Kinsale. Published in Riposte and other periodicals.

Durack, Michael *Exclusion Zone* P70, lives in Co.Clare, published in Poetry Ireland Review, Departures, Incognito, Riverine, Limerick Poetry Broadsheets 4 & 5, Flaming Arrows 1, 2 & 3, and RTE Radio 1.

Egan, Ann *Sliding Stones* P69, lives in Co. Kildare widely published.

Finan Hewitt, Marian *Soldier* P72, lives in Tallaght, won 1st prize in Riposte 1997, also prizes in Hopkins, widely published.

**Guckian, Mary** *In The Library,* P73, lives in Ringsend, has had work published in England, America and Australia. Her poems have also appeared in Books Ireland, Women's Work IX, Riposte and Extended Wings. Member of Rathmines Writers'Workshop.

**Hayes, Stella** *Black Mantilla,* P50,lives in Dublin, won 1st prize in Syllables, published in Riposte and several other periodicals.

**Herron, Michael** *Song of the Cidermen,* P39, lives in Co. Kildare, won 1st prize in Gerard Many Hopkins also 1st. prize in Syllables, widely published.

**Hogan, Eithne** *Temper* P57, lives in Clondakin, teaches English, has won prizes in Hopkins published in Riposte and the Syllables Anthology.

**Hughes,Vera** *Land of Stone* P64 from Sligo, lives in Co.Westmeath Winner of The Coverdale Prize for Irish Poetry in 1993. Published in Riposte and several other periodicals, also published *The Strange Story of Sarah Kelly* in 1998.

**Kenny, Ita** *Cobwebs,* P51, lives in Churchtown, published in Riposte.

**Kirkpatrick, Daphne** *Paradise Lost* P47 lives in Cornwall, native of The Channell Islands, lived for a long time in Scotland, a teacher, is widely published.

**Ledwidge, Francis** *Thomas McDonagh* P 15, Killed in The Great War 1917, Complete Poems published 1997 by Goldsmith Press.

**MacDarby, Anne** *Blue Denim Boy* P66, lives in Kilkenny, native of Laois, won 1st prize Syllables 1995, has also won prizes in the Scottish International, published in Riposte, Extended Wings and several other anthologies

**Maguire, Mary** *Kiritimati Island,* P52, lives in Terenure, has won prizes in the Hopkins, widely published.

**McAteer, Maureen** , *Near Nirvana,* P 57, lives in Donegal, native of Limerick, Winner of Magill Summer School, also received prizes in Allingham Arts, and The Scottish International. Published in Riposte, Women's Work and read this poem on UTV in 1996.

**McCloskey, Phil** *Shadowless* P58. Born in Kerry, lives in Donegal. Founder member of Killybegs Writers' Workshop. Won the John Player Trophy,and the McGill Poetry Competition 1986 and 1987. .Published widely, broadcast on RTE. An established artist.

**McDonagh, Thomas** *The Yellow Bittern* P14. Executed 1916, one of the seven signatories of The Proclamation of Independence, Complete Poems published in 1916 by The Talbot Press.

**McEvoy, Alice** *Regrowth,* P58, lives in Belfast, lectures in Communication Skills and Creative Writing in the Belfast Institute of Higher Education. Published in the Cherrybright Anthology and Riposte.

**McGuirk, Phyllis** *How Could You?* P52, lives in Inchicore, published in Reality, Women's Works, appeared on Live at Three , RTE.

**Miller, Áine** *The Poet as Ikat Weaver,* P36, lives in Churchtown, Winner of the Kavanagh Award, also 1st prize in Riposte 1996, teaches creative writing, broadcasts on local radio, widely published, first collection, *Goldfish in a Babybath* by Salmon.

**Milton, John** *Paradise Lost* P11, father of English poetry.

**Moore, Patrica Anne** *Rage* P 66, lives in Co. Clare, formerly from Belfast, widely published, a professional in the field of Life Long Learning.

**Murphy, June** *Token of Love* P60, lives in Longford, joined Granard Writers' in 1989, published in Womens' Works, Waterford Review, Acorn 5, Beneath the Moate Vol. I & II and Riposte.

**Murray, Tommy** *Afterbloom* P55 Winner of The Kavanagh Award *1987,* has also won prizes in Syllables, Hopkins, Allingham and Nora Fahy. Poems featured in UTV documentary on the Valley of the Kings.

**O 'Meara, Liam,** *Someone Big is Dead* P44, *Neighbours* P53, *The Smart Missile* P67 Founder of Syllables, Editor of *The Complete Poems* of Francis Ledwidge, winner of Tipperary '96, Hopkins '97, Riposte '98, has also won prizes in The Scottish International and has had a poem published in the Wall Street Journal. Published in several anthologies.

O'Mahony, Nessa *Getting There* P63, lives in Dublin. Her poetry has appeared, Irish, UK, Italian and American periodicals, her first collection, "Bar Talk," Italics Press was published in 1999. Won the National Woman's Poetry Competition, short-listed for The Hennessy Award and the Kavanagh Award. Member Dublin Writers' Workshop.

Plunket, Joseph Mary *I see his Blood* P13, Executed 1916, one of the seven signatories of the Proclamation of Independence, Complete Poems published 1916 by The Talbot Press.

Sempers, Ann, *Casulty,* P68, lives in Palmerstown, won 1st prize in Chapter and Verse, also prizes in Hopkins and Tipperary. Published in Riposte, Reality, Women's Work and in the Syllables Anthologies.

Somerville-Large, Gillian *St Kevin,* P62, lives in Co. Kilkenny, widely published.

Sullivan, Breda *A Benediction,* P60, lives in Co. Westmeath, won 1st prize in Syllables also prizes in the Scottish International and Hopkins, published in Riposte and numerous other periodicals, first collection *After the Ball* by Salmon.

Vial ,Noelle *The Spring Clean* P51, lives in Donegal, winner of the Hennessy Award, published in America, widely published in Ireland.

Wallace, Maria *Lunch Out,* P71, lives in Fortunestown, won prizes in Dun Laoghaire Poetry Competition in English and Spanish sections, also in Hopkins, widely published, an artist in stained glass.

Wordsworth,William *The Daffodils* P7, the greatest lyrical poet of all time.

Young Jeremy, *The Speech Before Words,* P54, lives in Rathgar, won prizes in Riposte, published in Extended Wings and other periodicals.

# About the Author

Michael O'Flanagan is the editor of the poetry broadsheet *Riposte,* which was launched in 1996 and which now has members in Ireland, England, Germany, France, Italy, Belgium, America, Canada, Korea and Malta. A member of the Inchicore Writers' Group, *Syllables,* he is a former editor of *The Inchicore Times* and secretary of *The Francis Ledwidge Society.* In 1997 he published a biography of Henry Joy McCracken which was warmly received in America. As chairman of *The Kilmainham Arts Conference* he has facilitated three major group art exhibitions, at St. Mary's Abbey Henry St. in 1992, at Kilmainham Jail in 1994 and at The Bank of Ireland Arts Centre, Foster Place in 1996. During the 1998 bi-centenary commemorations of the 1798 Rebellion he organised the erection new commemorative plaques to Lord Edward Fitzgerald, at St. Werburghs Church and to John and Henry Sheares at St. Michan's Church, in conjunction with Dublin Tourism and The Dublin '98 Committee. He has previously published two collections of his poetry, *Immutability,* published in 1991 and *Peep into the Abyss* published in 1993. He has broadcast his poetry on several local radio stations in the Dublin area and much of his work has also been included in the Syllables anthologies.

## Funding

*I know The Arts Council,*
*But they, don't know me,*
*So the chances of funding*
*are zero - by three!*

This publication receives no support from The Arts Council